A Time to Hide

Based on a True Story of Survival During the Holocaust

Marion Seidemann Fredman

Art by
Elisa Kleven,
Diane Dove, and
Juliana Fredman

Library of Congress Cataloging-in-Publication Data available.

978-1-685556280
ebook 978-1-685558864
LCCN: 2024919290

Manufactured in China.

Editor: Rebekah Lovato Piatte.
Design by Andrea Kelly.
Art by Elisa Kleven [front cover, pp. 16-17, 30 (left), 36 (left), 38-39, 40 (top), 45, 54-55, 58 (top left), 60, 63, 71, 74, 92-93]; Diane Dove [pp. 3, 8 (bottom right), 12-13 (left), 19 (top right), 24, 30-31(right), 36-37 (right), 40 (bottom), 41, 42 (left), 43 (top), 52 (top), 57, 58-59 (right), 70 (left)] and Juliana Fredman [pp. 28-29, 48, 51, 72-73].
Additional Illustrations: Marion Seidemann Fredman: pp. 34-35, 69; Bob Pannekoek : pp. 66, 70 (top right), 88-89.
Author Photograph by Clara Rice.

All images from the collection of Marion Seidemann Fredman, except for:
pp. 2-3, 60: MM_photos/shutterstock.com; p. 4: Minakryn Ruslan/shutterstock.com; pp. 4-5: Ilopa/shutterstock.com; p. 6: GEORGIOS TZIAROS/shutterstock.com; p. 7: Andreas Wolochow/shutterstock.com; pp. 7, 63: Photo_123/shutterstock.com; pp. 8, 22, 82-87, 90-91, 94-96: Here/shutterstock.com; pp. 8, 9: National Digital Archives, CC BY-SA 4.0, via Wikimedia Commons; p. 10: Bokeh Blur Background/shutterstock.com; pp. 11, 32, 53: Everett Collection/shutterstock.com; p. 11: Tartezy/shutterstock.com; shell_s/shutterstock.com; p. 12-13: VBVVCTND/shutterstock.com; p. 13: Massimo Vernicesole/shutterstock.com; malven57/shutterstock.com; pp. 14-15: Antiqua Print Gallery/Alamy; p. 18: Papin Lab/shutterstock.com; p. 19: Mateusz Atroszko/shutterstock.com; pp. 19, 19, 57, 89: David M. Schrader/shutterstock.com; pp. 20-21: Rawpixel.com/shutterstock.com; p. 22: Locomotive74/shutterstock.com; p. 23: United States Holocaust Memorial Museum, courtesy of National Archives and Records Administration, College Park; IHX/shutterstock.com; Katerina Maksymenko/shutterstock.com; p. 24: Chinnapong/shutterstock.com; pp. 25, 77: Jonas Vegele/shutterstock.com; pp. 26-27: Lial/shutterstock.com; pp. 27, 82: Prokrida/shutterstock.com; p. 27: denispro/shutterstock.com; p. 28: Wisutti/shutterstock.com; pp. 30-31: Jeffrey Schmieg/shutterstock.com; pp. 32-35: OlegRi/shutterstock.com; p. 33: Yellow "Star of David" badge, Netherlands, 1942-1945, printed cotton, The Magnes Collection of Jewish Art & Life, UC Berkeley, 78.11.2; pp. 40-41: Mappingz/shutterstock.com; pp. 42-43: Maly Designer/shutterstock.com; pp. 44, 70: Karuntana999/shutterstock.com; p. 44: Maarten van Gilse (left) and Walter Brandligt (right) forging identity cards. Photographer: Violette Cornelius, Uploader: Jonne Brandligt, CC0, via Wikimedia Commons; p. 45: Eka's studio/shutterstock.com; pp. 46-47: Annmarie Young/shutterstock.com; pp. 48-49: Clari Massimiliano/shutterstock.com; pp. 50, 56: Ganjalex/shutterstock.com; pp. 52-53: Only background/shutterstock.com; p. 52: Mark Anthony Ray/shutterstock.com; pp. 54-55: Ceren Bayrak/shutterstock.com; p. 60: MM_photos/shutterstock.com; p. 61, endpapers: Robin Kay/shutterstock.com; p. 62: HaxVer/shutterstock.com; pp. 64-65, 68: Matveev Aleksandr/shutterstock.com; pp. 66-67: Seda Aydogdu/shutterstock.com; p. 71: APugach/shutterstock.com; pp. 74-75: JOJOSTUDIO/shutterstock.com; p. 76: Jizu/shutterstock.com; pp. 78-79: Luria/shutterstock.com; p. 78: Detroit Photographic Co. *Statue of Liberty, New York Harbor.* New York State New York New York Harbor United States, ca. 1905. Photograph. https://www.loc.gov/item/2008679689/; fogcatcher/shutterstock.com; pp. 80-81: Tetiana A/shutterstock.com; The Miriam and Ira D. Wallach Division of Art, Prints and Photographs: Photography Collection, The New York Public Library. (1902 - 1913). View of the Immigration Station, Ellis Island (front side). Retrieved from https://digitalcollections.nypl.org/items/31031090-c6da-012f-d2f8-58d385a7bc34; p. 86: Sichon/shutterstock.com; pp. 88-89: David M. Schrader/shutterstock.com; Additional credits: AKAISER/shutterstock.com; LiliGraphie/shutterstock.com.

10 9 8 7 6 5 4 3 2 1

The Collective Book Studio®
Oakland, California
www.thecollectivebook.studio

Dedicated to my parents, Julius and Grete,
to the heroes who saved their lives and allowed me
to have one, and with great love to my children and
grandchildren, who make it all worthwhile:
Peter, Arden, Juliana, Gabe, Celia, Anabel, Dorian,
Felix, Sadie, Emmet, Julius, Jupitrr, and Daisy.

Never again for anyone.

BOCHUM, GERMANY. 1937.

Grete was twenty-six years old when she and her mother went to the synagogue on Rosh Hashanah. After the service, a handsome older man came over to introduce himself.

"Julius Seidemann."

"Grete Benjamin," she said.

Grete was delicate, with pale skin and clear, blue eyes.

Julius was large and sturdy, with an olive complexion and twinkling brown eyes.

They shook hands that day and smiled.

Grete was born in Bochum and could trace her family back to the 1500s.

Julius served as a soldier for Germany in World War I.

They were married five weeks later.

It was a hard time to be a Jew in Germany.

In 1937, the Nazi political party, led by Adolf Hitler, controlled the German government. For the last four years, Hitler had blamed the Jews for problems that the German people were facing. He spoke at rallies preaching messages of hate. Anybody who had different views became an enemy.

At first, Julius thought it was all just talk. *Who would take this man seriously?*

Surely nobody would listen to the horrible things Hitler said.

But they did.

They burned books written by Jews.

They banned Jews from teaching and going to school.

German citizens were encouraged to boycott Jewish shops and businesses . . .

including Julius's clothing stores.

Jewish and non-Jewish people also weren't allowed to marry. Julius's brother, Bruno, felt this personally. His girlfriend Ria was not Jewish and their relationship was considered a serious crime. So, she left Germany and went to Holland. They had both hoped this would be temporary and that she would be able to return home soon or he would be able to join her in Holland.

It didn't stop there.

The Nazis declared that Jews were no longer citizens of Germany. Jewish soldiers were kicked out of the army. Jewish doctors weren't allowed to treat patients or practice medicine in hospitals.

Hitler's message was loud and clear:
If you were Jewish, you weren't German.
If you were Jewish, you did not belong.

Grete and Julius felt threatened everywhere they went. They hoped people would speak out in their defense.

But they didn't.

When Grete and her Jewish friends were no longer allowed to go to the theater, their non-Jewish friends and colleagues watched—maybe they were sad or angry, but they said and did nothing. They were afraid. Grete and Julius were afraid, too.

A year passed. Things got worse.

Germany had always been home to Grete, but now she wanted to leave. As sad as it made her, Bochum wasn't a safe place anymore.

Julius thought they should stay. His clothing stores were doing well, despite the boycotts. If they left, how would they make money?

Besides, he reasoned, everything was already pretty bad, but they were still okay. How much worse could things get?

They decided to visit Holland where Julius's nephew Peter was staying with Ria. Peter had attended a German school for bright young men before he was expelled for being Jewish.

What if they visited him for his birthday?

Peter Jacobsohn would later escape Europe for Manchester, England, on a *Kindertransport* (children's transport).

Leaving Germany and the Nazis, even for a short while, would be a relief. Julius shared the plan with Bruno, who said he would join them there.

Grete and Julius packed a bag, crossed the border, and were welcomed into Holland.

They were happy to see Peter and Ria. After lots of hugs, they sat down to talk and share news.

Suddenly, the door opened and Bruno rushed in, sweating and breathless.

"We can't go back to Germany," he managed to say. "They know who we are."

Ehefrau

Lichtbild

Unterschrift des Paßinhabers

und seiner Ehefrau

Es wird hiermit bescheinigt, daß der Inhaber die durch das obenstehende Lichtbild dargestellte Person ist und die darunter befindliche Unterschrift eigenhändig vollzogen hat.

Bochum, den 11. Jan. 1935

Der Polizei-Präsident in Bochum

I.A.

2

PERSONENBESCHREIBUNG

		Ehefrau
Beruf	Kaufmann	
Geburtsort	Bialla	
Geburtstag	23. 7. 1904	
Wohnort	Bochum	
Gestalt	groß	
Gesicht	rund	
Farbe der Augen	braun	
Farbe des Haares	dunkelblond	
Besond. Kennzeichen	keine	./.

KINDER

Name	Alter	Geschlecht

3

Bruno told them he didn't have the official papers needed to cross from Germany into Holland, so he had used fake ones. The *Grenzpolizei* (border police) examined them and immediately knew something was wrong.

The Grenzpolizei tried to grab Bruno, but Bruno panicked. He punched the officer who grabbed him and ran as fast as he could.

Once Bruno ran across the border, the Dutch guard there stopped the German officer. “This man is on Dutch soil,” the Dutch guard said. “You can’t follow him here.”

ARNHEM, HOLLAND 1938

Grete and Julius enjoyed their short time in Holland. They had almost forgotten what it was like to walk around without feeling like someone was watching their every move.

They were still aware of the growing threat in Germany, though. Ria's older brother was in the United States, so Ria and Bruno were able to immigrate there thanks to his sponsorship. They said their goodbyes to Julius and Grete—looking forward to the time they would meet again.

"We should stay in Holland," Grete said to her husband the night before they planned to travel back to Bochum. "I could bring my mother."

"We'll need to get some things from home," he said.

Because of Bruno's eventful border crossing, it wasn't safe for Julius—with the same last name—to cross the border. But Grete's papers didn't have the Seidemann name, so she had a better chance of returning to Germany unnoticed.

The next day, she was ready to leave.

"Don't worry, I'll be fine," she said as she kissed Julius goodbye. "I'll be back soon."

Grete Benjamin

Bochum had gotten even worse.

When Grete arrived at one of Julius's stores, she discovered it no longer belonged to him. The Nazis had taken possession of the shop, even though Julius and Grete had been gone only a short time. They wouldn't let her take money from the register and forced her to leave.

The bank refused to help. They had closed her and Julius's accounts, so she left empty-handed.

When Grete arrived at their apartment, she saw that it was a mess. It had been ransacked.

She grabbed what she could, shoving clothes and other items into her bag.

There wasn't much left.

Their driver had even taken Julius's beloved car.

The cook had buried some silverware and keepsakes in the yard and promised to give them back to Grete when it was safe.

But when would that be?

Cilly Benjamin, Grete's mother, was a widow in her late fifties. She lived near her sister, Frieda, and had many friends in the neighborhood.

Grete hurried to her mother's home. It would not be easy to convince her mother and aunt to leave, but Grete had to try.

When the door opened, Grete hugged her mother.

"Come with me to Holland," she said urgently. "Germany isn't safe."

Cilly shook her head. "Tyrants don't live forever."

"Mother, please!"

Her mother pressed her daughter's hand gently. "Don't worry about me," Cilly said. "Go with your husband. I'll be okay. We'll see each other when things are normal again."

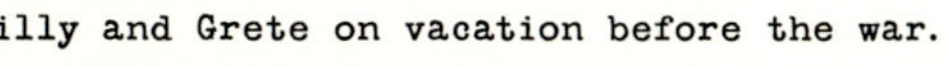

Cilly and Grete on vacation before the war.

Frieda Jacob and her daughter, Thea.

Grete returned to Holland alone. She never saw her mother or aunt again.

VELP, HOLLAND. 1938.

Grete and Julius found a sweet little house in the village of Velp. They became close to their neighbors, who soon felt like family to them.

Grete especially loved talking and laughing with Mies, who lived just down the street with her husband, Bob. Mies's voice boomed when she spoke. She told loud jokes and read tarot cards.

Mies and Grete quickly became dear friends. They often took walks and shared a *gezellig kopje thee* (a cozy cup of tea) in the afternoons.

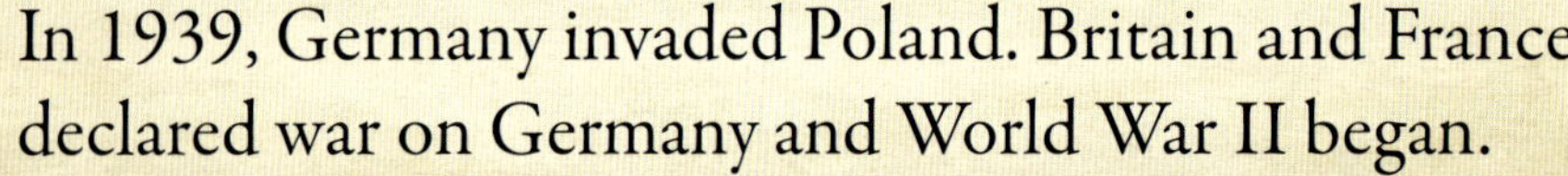

In 1939, Germany invaded Poland. Britain and France declared war on Germany and World War II began.

A year later, the Germans invaded and occupied Holland. The Nazis now controlled most of Europe, including Poland, France, Austria, Belgium, Denmark, Greece, Norway, and the Netherlands. It seemed like there was no stopping Germany.

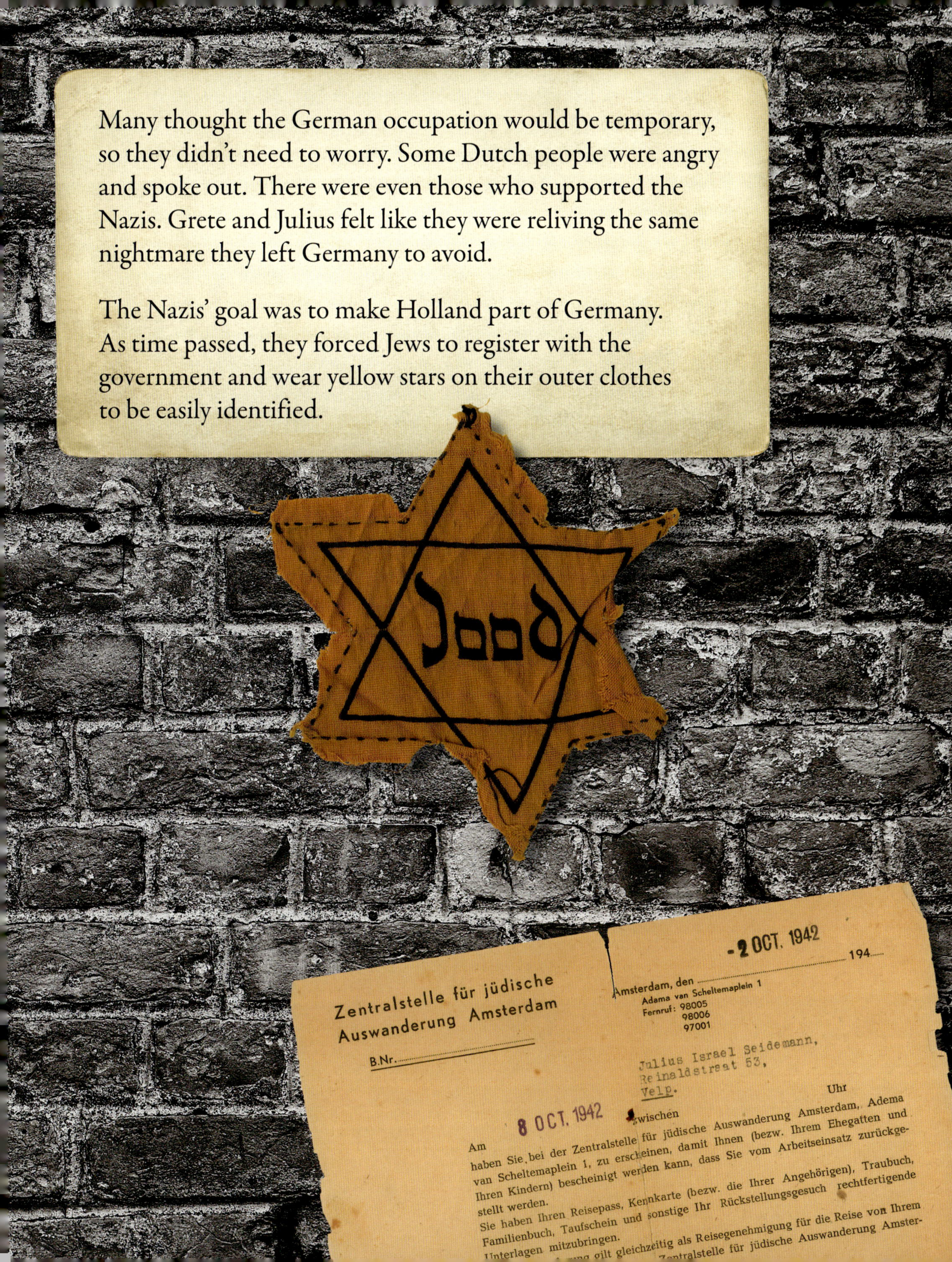

Many thought the German occupation would be temporary, so they didn't need to worry. Some Dutch people were angry and spoke out. There were even those who supported the Nazis. Grete and Julius felt like they were reliving the same nightmare they left Germany to avoid.

The Nazis' goal was to make Holland part of Germany. As time passed, they forced Jews to register with the government and wear yellow stars on their outer clothes to be easily identified.

Zentralstelle für jüdische
Auswanderung Amsterdam

B.Nr. ....

Amsterdam, den -2 OCT. 1942 194....
Adama van Scheltemaplein 1
Fernruf: 98005
98006
97001

Julius Israel Seidemann,
Reinaldstraat 53,
Velp.

Am 8 OCT. 1942 zwischen Uhr

haben Sie bei der Zentralstelle für jüdische Auswanderung Amsterdam, Adema van Scheltemaplein 1, zu erscheinen, damit Ihnen (bezw. Ihrem Ehegatten und Ihren Kindern) bescheinigt werden kann, dass Sie vom Arbeitseinsatz zurückgestellt werden.

Sie haben Ihren Reisepass, Kennkarte (bezw. die Ihrer Angehörigen), Traubuch, Familienbuch, Taufschein und sonstige Ihr Rückstellungsgesuch rechtfertigende Unterlagen mitzubringen.

... gilt gleichzeitig als Reisegenehmigung für die Reise von Ihrem ... Zentralstelle für jüdische Auswanderung Amster-

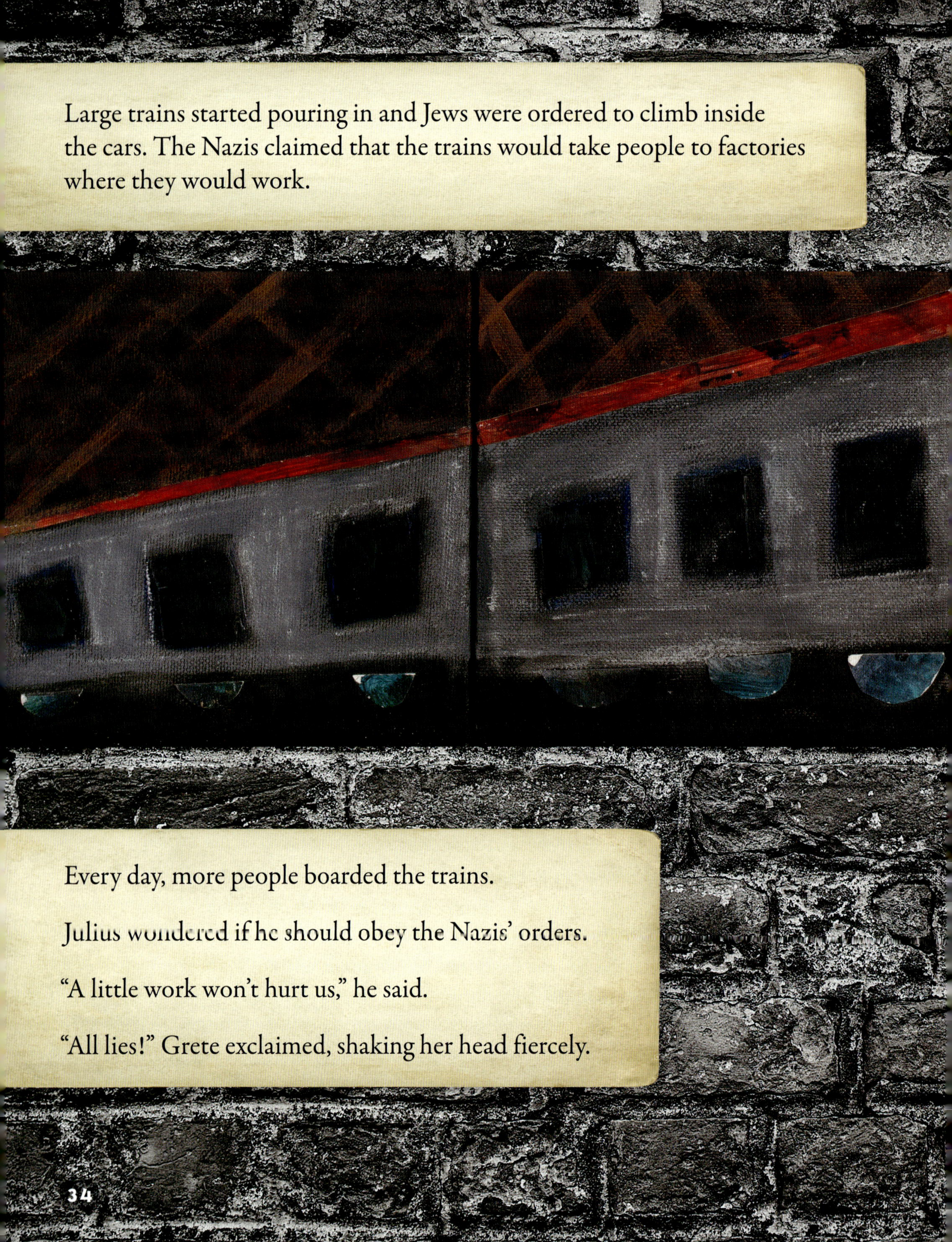

Large trains started pouring in and Jews were ordered to climb inside the cars. The Nazis claimed that the trains would take people to factories where they would work.

Every day, more people boarded the trains.

Julius wondered if he should obey the Nazis' orders.

"A little work won't hurt us," he said.

"All lies!" Grete exclaimed, shaking her head fiercely.

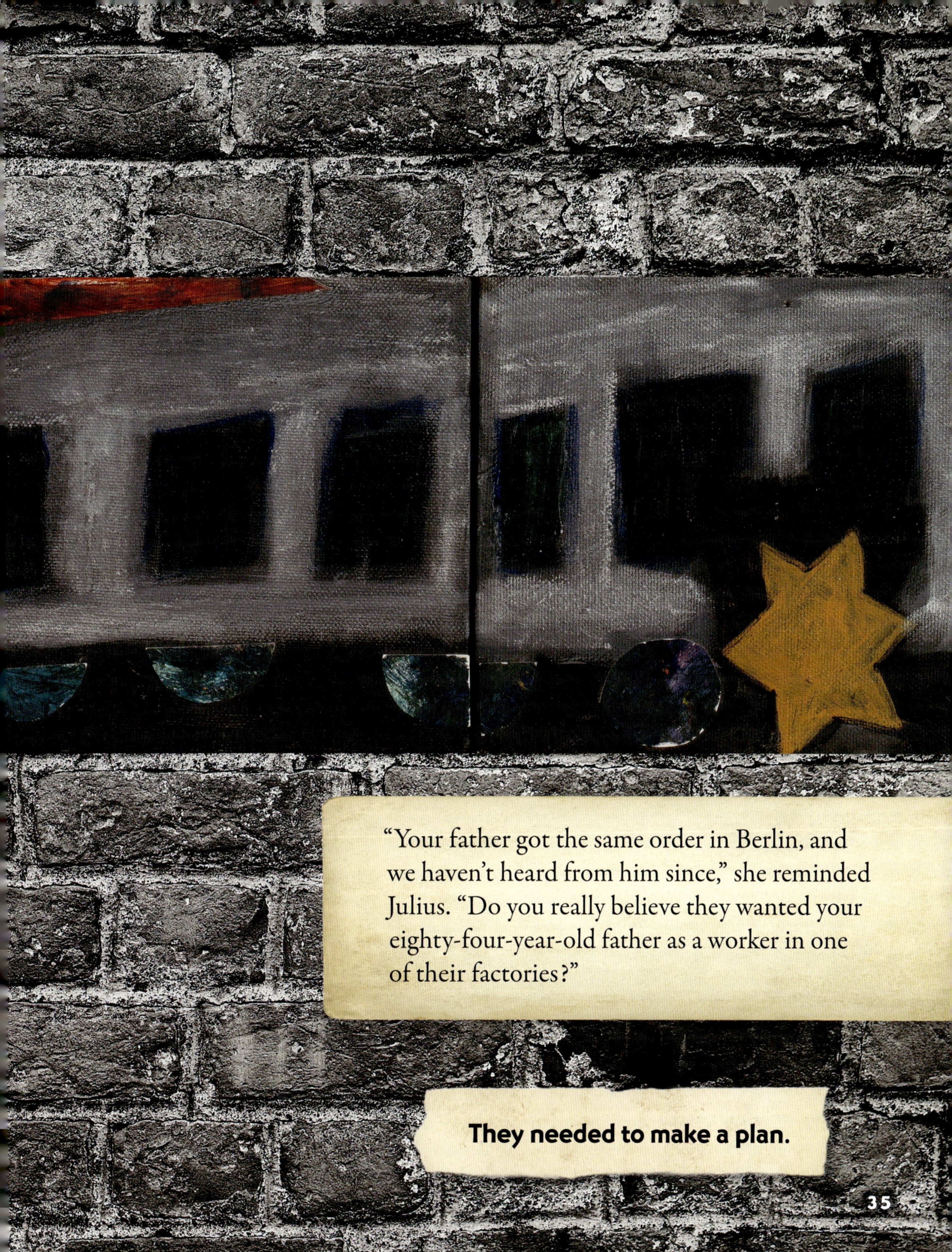

“Your father got the same order in Berlin, and we haven’t heard from him since,” she reminded Julius. “Do you really believe they wanted your eighty-four-year-old father as a worker in one of their factories?”

They needed to make a plan.

It was hardest to tell Mies.

"Onderduiken (go into hiding). We need to hide—just for a while—until the Nazis leave Holland. We have a place to go. It's all arranged," Grete said.

"Where?"

"I can't tell you where."

"When?"

"I can't tell you when. One day we'll just disappear."

Mies began to cry. It was too dangerous for her to know. She was going to miss Grete so much. But even more than that, she was afraid for her friend. She tried to smile through her tears—to be brave for Grete.

One cold winter night, Grete and Julius quietly left their cozy home. They tore the yellow stars off their clothing, dropped them in the garbage, boarded a train, and disappeared into the darkness.

APELDOORN, HOLLAND. 1942.

Nineteen miles from Velp, Tinie and Truss Heijmans, two sisters, lived in a big house on Regentesselaan.

Oftentimes, one of them would be traveling far away, doing missionary work, but when they came back, Regentesselaan was home.

Tinie and Truss went to church every week, where their priest spoke from the pulpit about the great evil happening in Europe. He said everyone must help if they could.

He asked Tinie and Truss to take a couple into their home.

They could have said no. It was scary. It was dangerous. The Nazis could arrest them—or worse.

But they said yes.

That was how a man with twinkling brown eyes and a woman with pale skin and blue eyes arrived, shivering, on the doorstep of their house.

Grete and Julius followed Tinie and Truss through the big house to the top of a long, narrow stairway. They opened the door to the small attic.

A drawing from the early plans of the house on Regentesselaan.

The ceiling sloped down low on each side of the room, so they could only stand up in the middle. The sisters had tried their best to make it feel cozy. There was a divan with a built-in pillow covered in flowered fabric, a table, two chairs, a small lamp, and a few eating utensils.

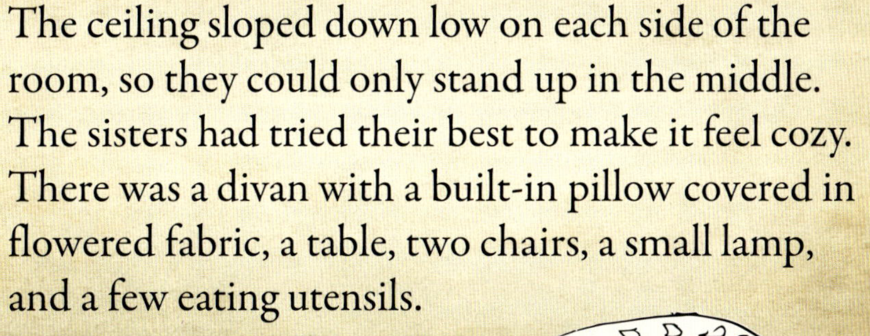

This was their home now. *But for how long?* Nobody knew. They knew only that the Nazis were searching for Jews in hiding and they needed to be very careful.

Julius pulled a small oriental rug out of his bag—a small comfort of home—and laid it on the floor near the divan.

They would make the best of it.

Not long after Grete and Julius moved in to the attic, a woman from the Dutch underground came to visit them.

The Dutch underground was a resistance group in Holland secretly fighting the Nazis in many different ways. They did a lot to help hide Jewish people.

"My name is Suzette," she said. She was pretty, with blond hair and honest, gray eyes. "I can't tell you much, and I can't stay long. But I will see you as often as possible and bring you things you need, like books, candles, soap, and news."

She looked around the attic and saw the windows. "Don't forget to be careful. Keep the curtains drawn. Don't let anyone see that you're up here. If anything happens, pretend I don't exist."

Grete and Julius nodded. Pretending not to exist was something they were learning to do themselves as well.

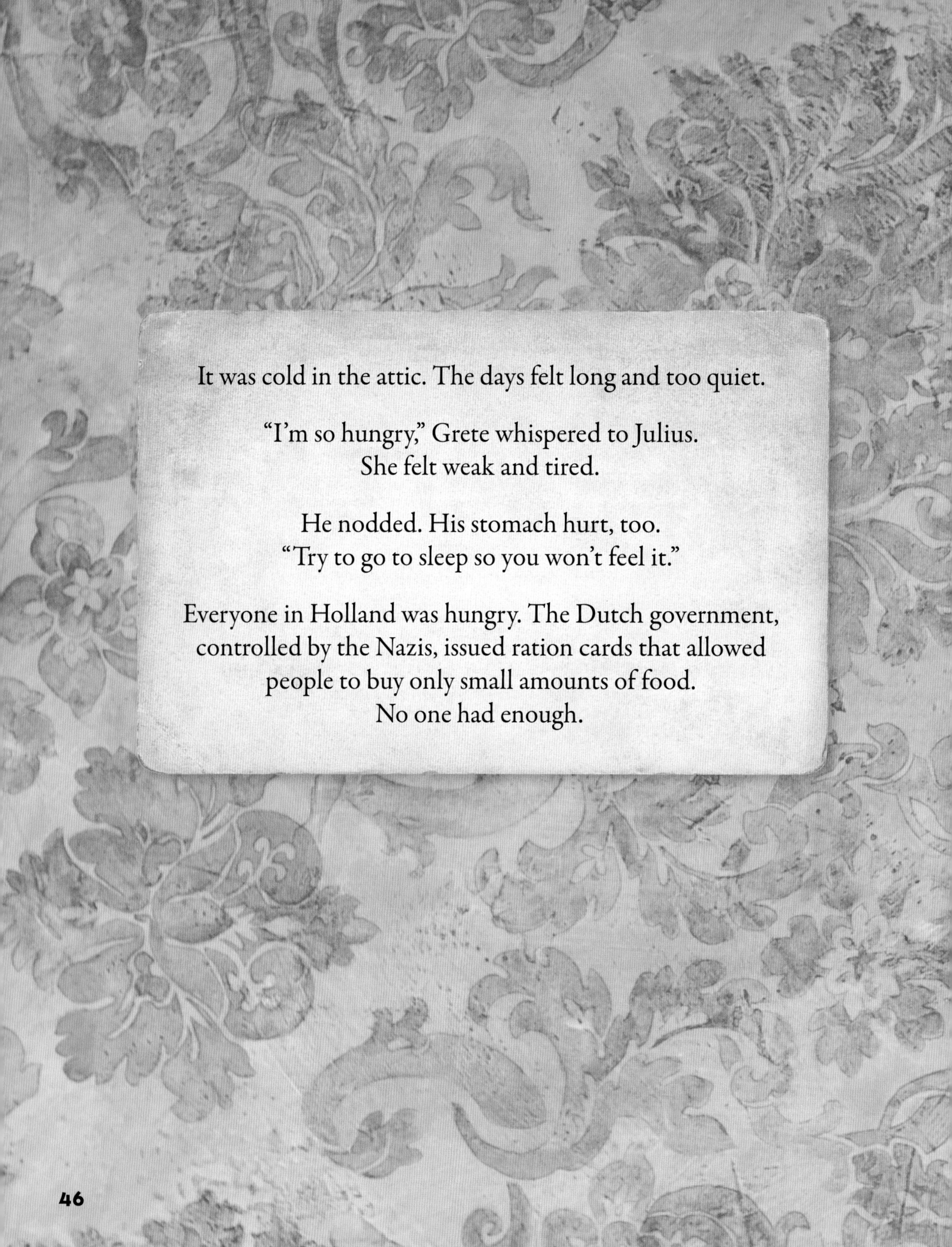

It was cold in the attic. The days felt long and too quiet.

"I'm so hungry," Grete whispered to Julius.
She felt weak and tired.

He nodded. His stomach hurt, too.
"Try to go to sleep so you won't feel it."

Everyone in Holland was hungry. The Dutch government, controlled by the Nazis, issued ration cards that allowed people to buy only small amounts of food.
No one had enough.

The Dutch underground made fake IDs and ration cards for Julius and Grete. The food wasn't much and it wasn't tasty, but Julius and Grete were grateful for it.

They lived like this for almost three years.

Every day they waited for news. Time dragged on.
They learned that it was important to keep busy to stay safe and sane.

"Haircut time," Grete said to Julius. Tinie had given them a small pair of barber scissors, and Grete was always deciding that Julius's hair and mustache needed trimming.

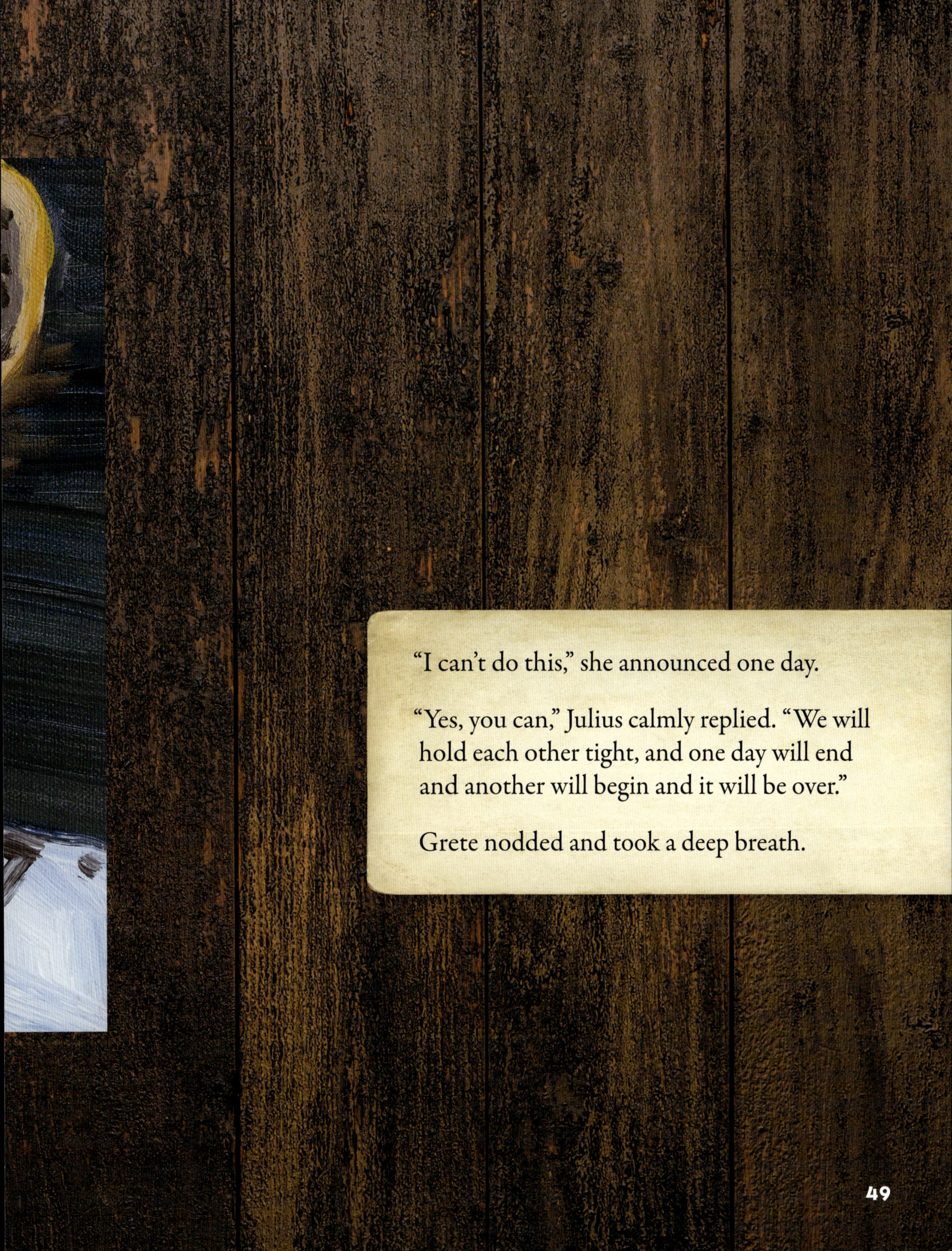

“I can’t do this,” she announced one day.

“Yes, you can,” Julius calmly replied. “We will hold each other tight, and one day will end and another will begin and it will be over.”

Grete nodded and took a deep breath.

"I want to dance," Grete sighed.

"What?"

"Let's dance."

"We don't have any music."

"We'll make our own."

"We'll have to be quiet."

"Okay."

They danced.

For a moment or an hour—perhaps hours—they forgot their fears.

APELDOORN, HOLLAND. 1944.

Sometimes Julius and Grete would go downstairs to hear the news on an old Philips radio. It was in English and difficult to understand because of the static. Their moods alternated between cautious hopefulness and total despair.

FINAL NIGHT EXTRA

THE SPIRIT OF A GREAT RACE LONG JOHN SCOTCH WHISKY

TUESDAY, JUNE 6, 1944

Still the Best! BIRD'S CUSTARD

Evening Standard

ONE PENNY

MOON Rises 9.50 pm; Sets 6.29 am.

37,357 BLACK-OUT 10.57 pm to 5.0 am

Churchill Announces Successful Massed Air Landings Behind Enemy in Franc

4000 SHIPS, THOUSAND

MALLER VESSELS

SHELLED

Meanwhile, the British, Canadians, Soviets, and Americans—also known as the Allies—helped the war against Germany by manufacturing tanks, guns, and planes. Young men all over the world trained and fought as soldiers.

Germany still occupied many countries like Holland, but their armies had been defeated in North Africa and Italy. The Soviets had overpowered them in Eastern Europe.

In June, Suzette was excited about the latest radio report.

"The Allies have landed in France. It's only a matter of days now," she told Grete and Julius.

Days passed. Then weeks. Then months. The Allied armies kept advancing, but the Nazi soldiers kept fighting back.

Grete started feeling sick. She was tired, nauseated, and achy. Julius was worried. "We need a doctor."

It was risky, but Suzette bravely arranged for a man named Dr. Forster to come in secret. No one was prepared for the news he had to give.

They looked at him in shock, certain they must have heard him wrong.

"Pregnant?" Grete repeated. "I can't have a baby," she said. "I have no home, no passport, no country. I'm stateless. I have no right to bring a baby into this world."

Surely the doctor could see that having a baby in this situation was impossible.

Dr. Forster disagreed.

"My dear," he said. He put his arm around her. "Do you know what's happening out there? Your people are being killed by the thousands, hundreds of thousands, maybe even millions. Men, women, and children. Babies." His voice was kind but serious. "Bringing a new Jewish life into the world is the greatest act of resistance against what the Nazis are doing. It is also the only hope for your people."

“But how can I carry a baby through this?”

“You won’t do it alone. I’ll be here to help you.”

Grete looked at him and Julius in the tiny attic room. She thought about Tinie, Truss, and Suzette.

The doctor was right.

She was not alone.

APELDOORN, HOLLAND. March 10, 1945.

Despite the Allies' advances in the war, Holland was still occupied and under Nazi control. Grete and Julius still lived in secret in the tiny attic. But their life was about to change, because Nazis or no Nazis, the baby was ready to be born.

Julius waited in the attic while Suzette took Grete with her false papers to a school that had been turned into a hospital for the German occupiers. Just as he had promised, the kind doctor was there.

A few hours later, Grete was holding a miracle in her arms, a healthy baby girl.

After the birth, Grete found herself sharing a room with the wife of a Nazi soldier. Grete was scared, but Dr. Forster was true to his word. She was not alone. He kept her identity a secret until she was able to take her new daughter home to Julius and the little attic room in the house on Regentesselaan.

APELDOORN, HOLLAND. March 26, 1945.

The baby was sixteen days old when
Nazi soldiers came to the house.

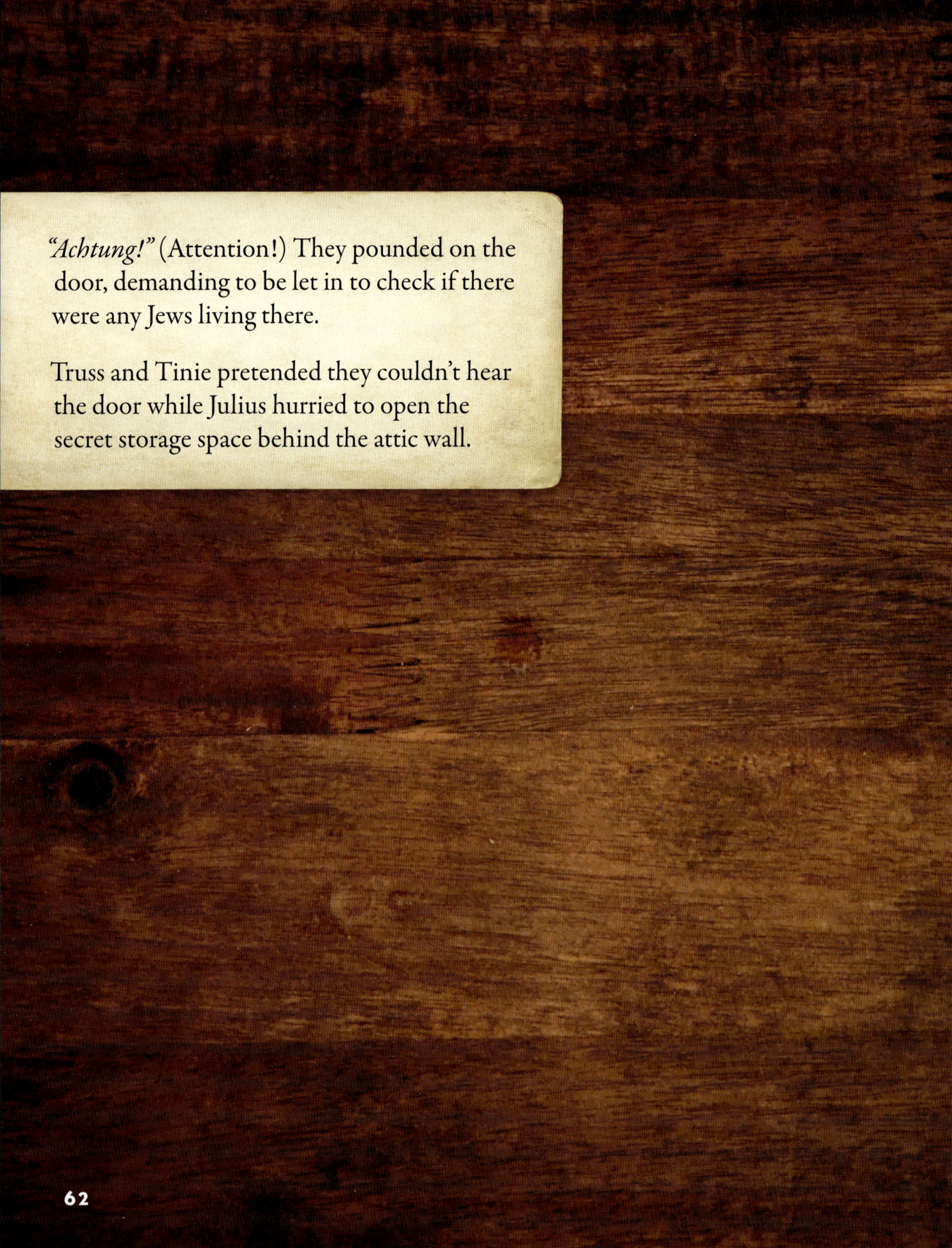

"Achtung!" (Attention!) They pounded on the door, demanding to be let in to check if there were any Jews living there.

Truss and Tinie pretended they couldn't hear the door while Julius hurried to open the secret storage space behind the attic wall.

Downstairs, Grete looked at the baby in her arms. They couldn't hide with her. If she cried, they would all be found and killed.

There was no time. Grete gently placed the baby in the bassinet and gave her a kiss. Then she went upstairs into the little space in the attic wall and stood next to Julius.

Truss and Tinie stalled for as long as they could. Finally, they opened the front door and the Nazis stormed in.

It was pitch black inside the wall. Julius and Grete could hear the Nazis searching the house below. Even though they were several floors up, every sound seemed magnified.

They thought they had a good hiding place. Grete and Julius hoped it would be enough and that they would be safe.

Then they heard a dog bark.

They froze.

If the Nazis had a dog with them, that was a very bad thing. The Nazis might not be able to see Julius and Grete hiding in the wall, but a dog could certainly smell them.

The dog and soldiers were getting closer. Grete and Julius tried to quiet the pounding of their hearts. They tried not to breathe.

26 Maart 1945.

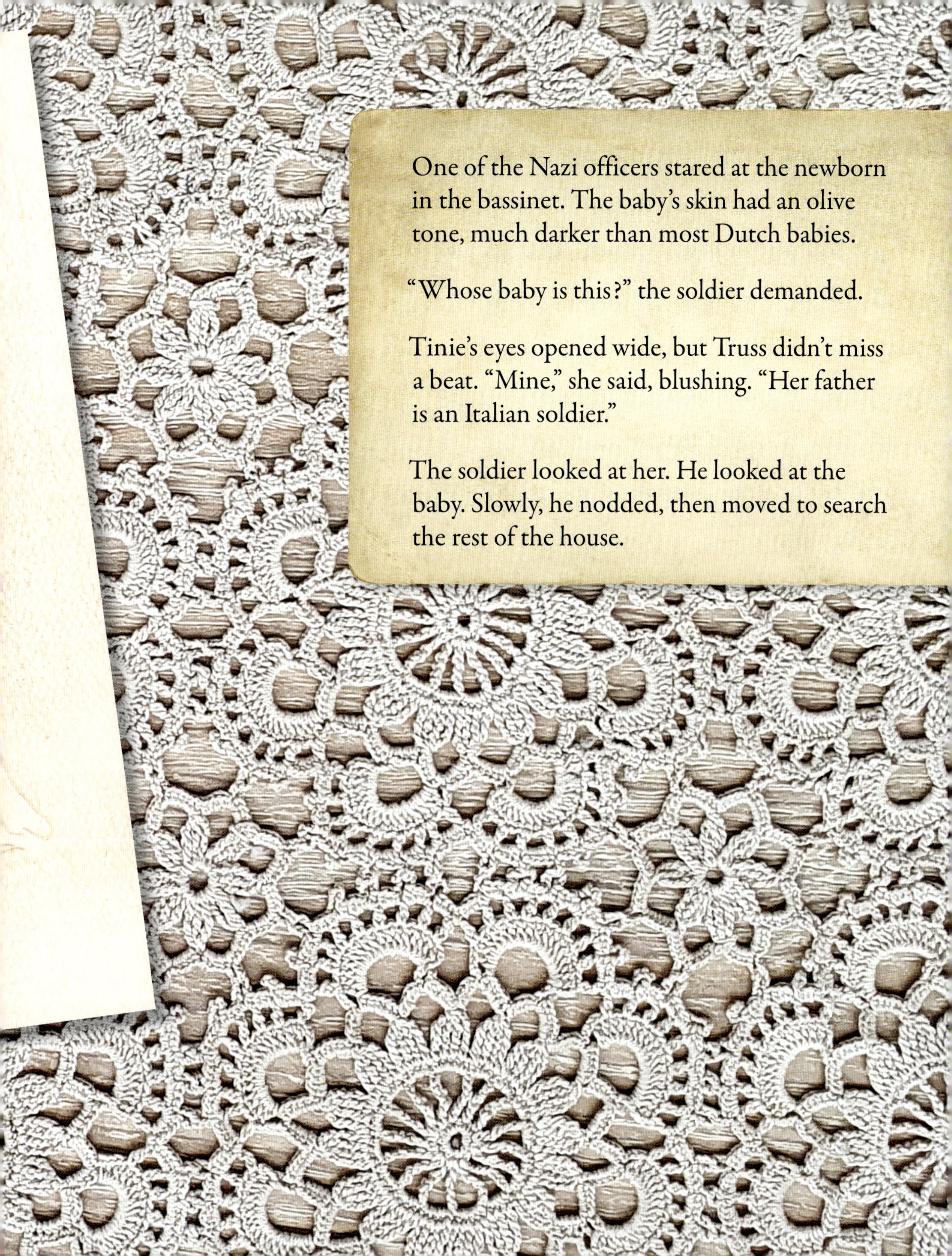

One of the Nazi officers stared at the newborn in the bassinet. The baby's skin had an olive tone, much darker than most Dutch babies.

"Whose baby is this?" the soldier demanded.

Tinie's eyes opened wide, but Truss didn't miss a beat. "Mine," she said, blushing. "Her father is an Italian soldier."

The soldier looked at her. He looked at the baby. Slowly, he nodded, then moved to search the rest of the house.

The Nazis looked under the beds and in the cupboards. They checked every corner of every room with their dog. The dog was specially trained to find people in hiding.

Grete and Julius knew the moment someone entered the tiny attic room. They couldn't see what was happening, but they could hear the soldiers searching. They could hear the dog.

In the dark, on the other side of the paneling, they held their breath. Staying as still as they could, they silently hoped with all the strength they could muster.

They hoped their daughter would be safe. They hoped Tinie and Truss would be safe. Suzette and the doctor, too. And they hoped for themselves.

The dog headed straight for where Julius and Grete were hiding. It sniffed the wall a few times. Then it turned and pulled its Nazi handler . . . out of the room and down the stairs.

Grete and Julius could not believe it.

The dog had saved them all.

APELDOORN, HOLLAND.
April 17, 1945.

The news spread everywhere. Canadian soldiers followed by Americans had reached Apeldoorn and defeated the Nazi forces.

Apeldoorn was liberated!

At six weeks old, tiny Marion Seidemann
blinked in wonderment out the window.
The streets were loud and filled with people.

After five long, hard years, the Dutch citizens were overjoyed to be free of the Nazis. People smiled, laughed, and drank champagne together, singing and dancing for as long as they wanted.

And right in the center of it all was Grete, dancing with them.

They could finally go home to Velp.

Mies let out a whoop of joy when she saw them walking back down the road. She swooped up Grete in her arms. The best friends reunited once again, this time with bigger families.

Julius, Grete, and Marion were taken in by an older Jewish man named *Meneer* (Mister) Cohn and his wife.

He was kind and even gave them bikes to move around town. Julius rode his bike everywhere with his daughter in the basket.

Marion liked living with the Cohns. They had big, beautiful Chow Chows who were so well trained that they wouldn't even eat a cookie if it was dropped out of the playpen.

Besides Bruno and Ria, Julius's sister Hannah and her family had also immigrated to the United States during the war. They had settled in St. Louis, Missouri. After liberation, the Red Cross contacted the family in Missouri and informed them that Grete, Julius, and little Marion had survived the war and were living in Velp, Holland.

By this time, Hannah's daughter Senta was married to a German-American soldier named Henry, who had been deployed to Europe. Senta and Hannah urged him to find the family. He took his mission seriously and went with the address on a crumpled piece of paper in his pocket to Velp, Holland. Once there, he approached a woman and asked for help in finding the address.

"*Bist du der Henry?*" he heard in return.

It was none other than Grete herself!

Henry and baby Marion.

Lieve Peter,
ik ben de jongste
nicht van jou en stuur je veel
lieve groeten en een hartelyke zoen!

Marion, Frederika,
Beatrise

Velp, September 1945

Grete announced Marion's birth to Peter with this postcard. Grete always said, "We went in with two and came out with three."

Julius and Grete were thrilled to be connected to family again. They decided they wanted to join them and applied to move to the United States. Bruno helped them. He promised the government in a document that he would take responsibility for the little family. It took nearly two years, but finally the applications were approved in 1947.

It was good news,
but it was also hard to leave.

United States of America

State of TENNESSEE
City of NASHVILLE
County of DAVIDSON } ss.:

I Robert Bruno Seideman - Born July 23, 1904, Bialla, Germany
age 42 being duly sworn, depose and say:

I reside at 3010 West End Avenue, Jacksonian Apartments, Nashville, Tennessee

I am a ~~Native American~~ or Naturalized Citizen of the United States as evidenced by (indicate which) my Naturalization Certificate No. 6396607 issued on January 22, 1945 by United States District Court at Nashville, Tennessee

I am married (married or single) and dependent on me for support are my wife

I am a traveling salesman for one of the Country's largest wash dress manufacturers - Boris Smoler & Sons, 3021 N. Pulaski Road, Chicago, Illinois, (State fully business or occupation, location, earnings) covering the states of Kentucky, Tennessee and West Virginia. My yearly earnings have never been less than $10,000.00 per year, ever since I started with my company five years ago.

In addition, I have assets consisting of $7,850.00 War Bonds + $18,338.42 in savings accounts - $1,142.81 balance in checking account. $514.49 life insurance cash value. (State investments, savings, life insurance, real property, etc.) 1941 Oldsmobile, cash value about $1100.00 - Home furniture, carpets, silver and glassware - cash value approximately $3500.00.

I am the brother (state relationship) of Julius Seidemann Born on June 16, 1892 in Johannisburg, Germany. (give names and ages of persons abroad) Brother-in-law of Grete Seidemann, born on April 16, 1911 in Bochum, Germany - Uncle of Marion FredericksaBeatrix Seidemann, born on March 10, 1945 in Apeldorn, Netherland.

now residing at 10 Arnhemschestreet, Velp (G), Netherlands

who desire to come to the United States to join me and others of the family, and whom I am most anxious to bring over.

I do hereby promise and guarantee that I will receive and take care of my relatives who are applying for an immigration visa, and will at no time allow them to become public charges to any community or municipality. I do further promise and agree that those of my relatives covered by this affidavit within school age will attend public school, and will not be permitted to work until they are of age.

I make this affidavit for the purpose of inducing the United States Consular authorities to grant the visa to my said relative , and herewith submit corroborative proof as to my personal standing.

Sworn to before me this 2nd day of January, 1946

Mary C. Mammarelli
Notary Public.
My Commission Expires JULY 7, 1949

Robert Bruno Seideman

Bruno's sworn and signed document, used in Julius and Grete's immigration application.

The goodbyes from the neighborhood were filled with tears and love. Mies and Grete hugged each other for a very long time. Julius thanked Meneer Cohn for all his kindness, and Meneer Cohn promised to take care of their bikes. The family packed their things and got ready to board a ship.

MS *Gripsholm*.

The family of three safely landed at Ellis Island in New York Harbor.

Germany held their roots, and Holland provided them refuge. But the United States would be their new home. They would reunite what was left of the family and move forward.

Author's Note

I was that baby, and Grete and Julius were my parents. From Holland, we got on the Swedish ship the MS *Gripsholm*, and on March 10, 1947, the three of us landed at Ellis Island in New York Harbor. Waiting to greet us with flowers and tears were my cousin Senta, Aunt Ria, and Uncle Bruno.

My parents never thought they'd leave Germany. They were deeply rooted and had many important relationships there.

The three of us shortly before we left Holland.

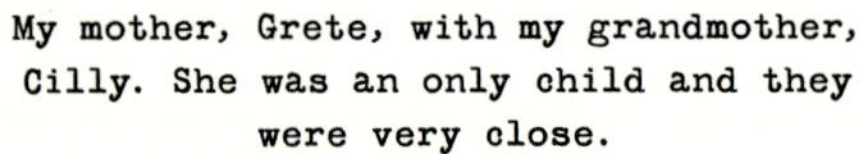

My mother, Grete, with my grandmother, Cilly. She was an only child and they were very close.

Mary was my mother's best friend from childhood. I always heard of their adventures together. Mary did not survive the war, and my mom felt her loss acutely.

My father was born in Biała, Prussia. He moved as a young man to Bochum, Germany, where there were more business opportunities.

My father and his brother Leo.

Here is the family in front of the family business in Biała. They made vinegar out of wheat. My father is on the far left and Uncle Bruno is on the far right.

My father was one of nine children. This photo was taken at the seventieth birthday of his father, Eduard Seidemann.

Me and my "two sets of parents."

Uncle Bruno and Aunt Ria were married in 1938 and settled in Nashville, Tennessee. They never had children and I spent summers with them. Growing up I thought I had two sets of parents.

My cousin Peter eventually came to the United States as well. He finished high school in Nashville while living with Ria and Bruno and ultimately got degrees from Vanderbilt and Northwestern. He never stopped trying to find his parents and sister.

Me, Peter, and my father posing for a photo on our very first roll of color film.

My father's brother Theo also survived the war. His family went to Chile in 1939.

Me and Tinie in 1973.

Tinie and Truss were two of many Dutch citizens who risked their lives to help Jews during the German occupation. My mother always stayed in touch and we visited when we could. Suzette and Dr. Forster were members of the Dutch underground, the organization my parents connected with when they went into hiding. Unfortunately, Suzette did not survive the war. I never found out what happened to Dr. Forster.

Family legend is that my father searched for the dog that saved our lives once we were out of hiding. From a tiny peephole through the wall, though, he was just barely able to see what it looked like. He said he wanted to adopt the dog—or at least buy it a steak—but was never able to find it.

Not all of my family made it out of Europe. In 1942, my grandmother Cilly Benjamin, and her sister, Frieda Jacob—along with Frieda's husband and daughter—were sent to a ghetto in Zamość, Poland. They died in a gas chamber in Bełżec. Julius's father, Eduard Seidemann, who was over eighty years old, was deported to the Bergen-Belsen concentration camp. He did not survive the journey. Many of Julius's siblings and their families were never seen again: Rosa and her son Heinz; Leo and his wife Elsa Taub; Frida and Erich Jacobsohn and their daughter, Inge (Peter's family).

These memorial stones are known as *"Stolperstein."* They are laid to memorialize victims of the Nazis. I was able to find and photograph some of my own lost family.

Peter Jacobsohn as a baby with his mother, Frida.

Peter's little sister, Inge. She was three years younger than him.

5
POND
3
ONS
26 Ma
Zaterdag
10 Maart 1945.
Geboren:
Marion Frederika Bea

Bob Pannekoek was an amazing artist, and he illustrated and put together my baby book—including this image that was used throughout the book.

In 1955, I was able to visit Holland and see Bob and Mies Pannekoek once again. Their sons became great adventure mates with whom I am still gratefully in touch.

That same year, we also visited the Budels who lived across the way from my parents in Velp, Holland. Ma and Pa Budel had a great vegetable garden, and Jan and Pauline were the nicest teenagers ever! They took ten-year-old me on bike rides and to the beach. It was magical and our families became forever bonded.

Shelling peas in the Budels' garden.

Top row, left to right: Grete, Ria, Senta. Bottom row, left to right: Uncle Max (Aunt Hannah's husband), Julius, and Aunt Hannah.

What I learned was "It's all everyone's business, and family is what matters."

I spent much of my childhood in St. Louis, Missouri. Our family of three lived across the street from my Aunt Hannah and her family. My father would stop by to see her every day.

A celebration in honor of my father's sixty-fifth birthday with family and friends.

In the 1950s, we received a box shipped from Germany to our new home in St. Louis. It included the silverware that the cook had buried. Over the years, we accumulated some more of our lost things—paintings, crystals, china, furniture, and more.

Some families didn't talk about the hard times, but my family did. They talked about it all—the good, the bad, the ugly. Still, so many details about my family's history are now lost. I wish I had asked more questions of the older generations but am grateful for what they've given me. The divan and rug that my parents had with them in the attic are alive and well. They sit on the floor of my dining room in my home in Berkeley, California.

Julius and Grete lived until 1972 and 1976, respectively. They spent the rest of their lives surrounded by love and family.

My mother and father with their first two grandchildren—my son Peter and daughter Arden—in 1971.

Looking back at all this, it becomes clear how acts of love and courage keep paying forward for generations.

Endnotes:

Page 4:
Rosh Hashanah: the Jewish New Year.

Page 9 & 11: *"Deutsche! Wehrt Euch! Kauft nicht bei Juden"* (German): Germans! Defend yourself! Don't buy from Jews!"

Page 15:
Kindertransport (German): Children's transport. An informal name for a series of rescue efforts between 1938 and 1940. The British government allowed unaccompanied children under the age of seventeen to enter their borders. About ten thousand children were brought to safety from the Nazis.

Page 18:
Grenzpolizei (German): Border police.

Unterschrift des Paßinhabers (German): Signature of the passport holder.

Page 20:
sponsorship: When someone agrees to take responsibility for or pay for something or someone else.

Page 31:
gezellig kopje thee (Dutch): *Gezellig* describes coziness and kinship with others, and *kopje thee* means "cup of tea."

Page 33:
Jood (Dutch): Jew. Nazis forced Jews to wear these yellow patches so they could easily be identified.

Zenstralstelle für jüdische Auswanderung Amsterdam(German): "Central Office for Jewish Emigration Amsterdam." This document called for Julius to appear before this office in charge of removing Jews from the country—ultimately calling to send him to the concentration camps under the guise of employment. Note that Julius also had to include the name "Israel" as his middle name—something all Jewish men were required to do by the Nazis.

Page 36:
Onderduiken (Dutch): To go into hiding.

This brooch was my grandmother Cilly's. You can see her wearing it on page 26, and I still wear it today.

Page 46:
ration card: A card of coupons people needed in order to buy food or other important items. The Nazis required a special identification card (shown on page 47) to use with the coupons to try to expose anybody hiding.

Page 62:
achtung (German): Attention.

Page 75:
Meneer (Dutch): Mister.

Page 76:
"*Bist du der* Henry?"(German): "Are you *the* Henry?"

Page 77:
"*Lieve Peter* . . ." (Dutch): "Dear Peter, I'm your youngest cousin and send much love and a heartfelt kiss."

Page 83:
Prussia: An area of Europe that later became part of Germany, Russia, and Poland.

Page 86:
concentration camp: a place where large numbers of people were imprisoned and forced to work or killed.

gas chamber: A room where poisonous gas could be used to kill many people.

Acknowledgments

First and foremost, I want to thank my husband, Steve Fredman, for his commitment to history collection, recording, storytelling, listening, remembering—and for being a never-ending source of knowledge and support.

Family and friends who have listened, proofread, commented, encouraged, and cheered me on: You know who you are. You've helped me so much.

I want to especially single out Marc Budel and thank him for his research and friendship.

I am so grateful for the many kids, grandkids, and friends who have included me in their school reports and projects and reminded me that it is important to tell our stories.

To the wonderful team at The Collective Book Studio, who have shepherded me with patience through this arduous process: Thank you.

Speaking of arduous: Thank you Arden for so much.

I also gratefully acknowledge the artists: my daughter Juliana and dear friends Elisa Kleven and Diane Dove. Your work has made every illustration meaningful to me.

Author Bio

Marion Seidemann Fredman lives in Berkeley, California, surrounded by her family, friends, dogs, chickens, treasures, and memories. She spends much of her time in her garden making whimsical art and hanging out with her offspring. This is her first book.

STATES IMMIGRANT INSPECTOR AT PORT OF A

States, or a part of another insular possession, in whatsoever class they travel, MUST be fully listed and the master or commanding officer of each

Arriving at Port of New York MARCH 10 1947

16	17	18			19	20	21	22				
No. on List	The name and complete address of nearest relative or friend in country whence alien came, or if none there, then in country of which a citizen or subject.	Final destination (Intended future permanent residence) Foreign country via (port of disembarkation)	In U. S. A. its territories or possessions State	City or town	Whether having a ticket to such final destination	By whom was passage paid? (Whether alien paid his own passage, whether paid by another person, or by any corporation, society, municipality, or government)	Whether in possession of $50, and if less, how much?	Whether ever before in the United States, and if so, when and where? (Last residence only) Yes or No	If Yes— Year or period of years	Where?	Date of last departure	Whether goi… friend; st… address,
1	Mother: Hildur Andersson, Sten-Stigen, Stenkyrka		Delaware	Wilmington	no	self	yes	no				Uncle: Adolf… 22 St. Wilm…
2	Mother: Anna Bassist, Ringvägen 83, Stockholm		Illinois	Chicago	no	self	yes	no				Fiancée: Mild… 13th Place,
3	Mother: Katarina Bamér, Västerlånggatan 27, Stockholm		Illinois	Chicago	yes	self	yes	no				Cousin: Ingeb… Baltmor, Chi…
4	Mother: Ester Berg, Essingestråket 16, St. Essingen		N.Y.	Long Island	no	self	$25	no				Friend: …helb… Valley, Long
5	Mother: Greta Söderlund, Styrmansgatan 38, Norrköping		N.Y.	Rye	no	self	yes	no				Friend: Doug… liam St. Rye
6	Mother: Valborg Hagton, Eriksbergsgatan 38, Stockholm		Ohio	Dayton	no	self	yes	no				Fiancée: Oliv… 2008 Stegmon…
7	Friend: Margareta Raab, Västmannagatan 30, Stockholm		N.Y.	New York	yes	self	yes	no				Mother: Annie… New York Cit…
8	....											
9	Mother: Blenda Sanden, Jungfrugatan 18, Stockholm		Illinois	Chicago	no	self	yes	no				Husband: Alla… Lawrence Ave…
10	Mother: Sara Kringlund, Regementsgatan 4, Strängnäs.		N.Y.	New York	yes	self	yes	no				Friend: Anne… ter Ave. Pate…
11	Sister: Katarina Johansson Sigtunagatan 11 Stockholm		Illinois	Chicago	yes	self	yes	yes	1925–1930	Chicago Ill.	Dec. 1930	Sister: Ebba… 1907 Wilson…
12	Brother: Eric Skuncke, Skuruvägen 5, Stocksund		Delaware	Claymont	no	self	yes	no				Brother: Carl… Claymont Gar…
13	....											
14	Friend: Miss Greta Andersson Herkulesgatan 22, Stockholm		Pa.	Wilkes Barre	no	self	yes	no				Wife: Malvin… Welles St. Wi…
15	Friend: Olof Dymling, Birger Jarlsgatan 24, Stockholm		N.Y.	New York	yes	self	yes	no				Cousin: Sam… 1501 "Fabian…
16	Mother: Anna Persson, Bäckmora Njutånger		N.Y.	New York	yes	self	yes	no				Sister: Viol… ler Pl. Broo…
17	Daughter: Heide Svensson Kananagatan 19 A, Västerås		Mass.	Worcester	no	self	$25	no				Friend: Geor… gamore Road,
18	Father: Mikael Ring Västmannagatan 15, Stockholm		N.Y.	New York	yes	self	yes	no				Uncle: Mendel… Gaw Pl. West…
19	Mother, Henny Dolley, 12 Queens Keep, Park Rd, Twickenham		Va.	Richmond	no	self	yes	no				Brother, We… 901 W. Frank…
20	Father, Meyertz Schenk, Snigel 273, Amsterdam		N.Y.	NewYork	yes	self	yes	no				Uncle, Will… 1803 Schene…
21	Father-in-law, do do		N.Y.	NewYork	yes	self	yes	no				Uncle, d…
22	Friend, Curt Wedel, 72 Gerard Doustraat, Amsterdam		N.Y.	White Plains	no	self	yes	no				Friend, Curt… 208 West Po…
23	Friend, do do		N.Y.	White Plains	no	self	yes	no				Friend,
24	Friend: L. Cohn, Arnhemsche Str. 10, Velp. Netherland		Tenn.	Nashville	no	see col. 23	yes	no				Brother, Br… 6 B. Jack So…
25	Friend: do do		Tenn.	Nashville	no	see col. 23	//	no				Brother-in-…
26	Friend: do do		Tenn.	Nashville	no	see col. 23	//	no				Uncle,
27	Father, Vaino Santavirta, Ylöjarvi		Conn.	Hartford	no	self	yes	yes	1922 1931	NewYork, N.Y.	Sept 23 1931	Friend, Wal… 23 Amity St…
28	Father-in-law, do do		Conn.	Hartford	no	husband	yes	no				Friend,
29	Friend: Oscar Front Backedal, Hellerup, Denmark.		N.Y.	NewYork	yes	self	yes	no				Friend: Vi… 89-25 190th…
30	Mother, Marie Jensen, Mellemvägen 64, Copenhagen		Pa.	Pittsburgh	no	self	yes	no				Husband, Bors… 607 Hay Str.

NOTE.—Full text of question 28 is as follows: Whether a person who believes in or advocates the overthrow by force or violence of the Government of the United St… or who disbelieves in or is opposed to organized government, or who advocates the assassination of public officials, or who advocates or teaches the unlawful destruction of… of or affiliated with any organization entertaining and teaching disbelief in or opposition to organized government or which teaches the unlawful destruction of property, or… the duty, necessity, or propriety of the unlawful assaulting or killing of any officer or officers, either of specific individuals or of officers generally, of the Government of th… other organized government because of his or their official character.